Grammar Minutes

Written by
Carmen S. Jones

Editor: Maria Elvira Gallardo, MA
Cover Illustrator: Rick Grayson
Cover Designer: Rebekah O. Lewis
Production: Karen Nguyen
Art Director: Moonhee Pak
Project Director: Stacey Faulkner

Table of Contents

Introduction

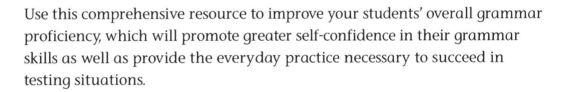

The main objective of *Grammar Minutes Grade 1* is grammar proficiency, attained by teaching students to apply grammar skills to answer questions effortlessly and rapidly. The questions in this book provide students with practice in the following key areas of first-grade grammar instruction:

- sentences
- nouns
- verbs
- adjectives
- pronouns
- contractions
- compound words
- synonyms
- antonyms
- articles

Use this comprehensive resource to improve your students' overall grammar proficiency, which will promote greater self-confidence in their grammar skills as well as provide the everyday practice necessary to succeed in testing situations.

Grammar Minutes Grade 1 features 100 "Minutes." Each Minute consists of 10 questions for students to complete within a short time period. As students are becoming familiar with the format of the Minutes, they may need more time to complete each one. Once they are comfortable and familiar with the format, give students a one- to two-minute period to complete each Minute. The quick, timed format, combined with instant feedback, makes this a challenging and motivational assignment that offers students an ongoing opportunity to improve their own proficiency in a manageable, nonthreatening way.

How to Use This Book

Grammar Minutes Grade 1 is designed to generally progress through the skills as they are introduced in the classroom in first grade. The Minutes can be implemented in either numerical order, starting with Minute 1, or in any order based on your students' specific needs during the school year. The complexity of the sentences and the tasks within each skill being covered gradually increase so that the first Minute of a skill is generally easier than the second Minute on the same skill. Review lessons are included throughout the book, as well as in an application section at the end of the book.

Grammar Minutes Grade 1 can be used in a variety of ways. Use one Minute a day as a warm-up activity, skill review, assessment, test prep, extra credit assignment, or homework assignment. Keep in mind that students will get the most benefit from each Minute if they receive immediate feedback.

If you use the Minute as a timed activity, begin by placing the paper facedown on the students' desks or displaying it as a transparency. Use a clock or kitchen timer to measure one minute—or more if needed. As the Minutes become more advanced, use your discretion on extending the time frame to several minutes if needed. Encourage students to concentrate on completing each question successfully and not to dwell on questions they cannot complete. At the end of the allotted time, have the students stop working. Read the answers from the answer key (pages 108–112) or display them on a transparency. Have students correct their own work and record their scores on the Minute Journal reproducible (page 6). Then have the class go over each question together to discuss the answers. Spend more time on questions that were clearly challenging for most of the class. Tell students that some skills that seemed difficult for them will appear again on future Minutes and that they will have another opportunity for success.

Teach students the following strategies for improving their scores, especially if you time their work on each Minute:

- leave more challenging items for last
- come back to items they are unsure of after they have completed all other items
- make educated guesses when they encounter items with which they are unfamiliar
- ask questions if they are still unsure about anything

Students will ultimately learn to apply these strategies to other assignments and testing situations.

The Minutes are designed to assess and improve grammar proficiency and should not be included as part of a student's overall language arts grade. However, the Minutes provide an excellent opportunity to identify which skills the class as a whole needs to practice or review. Use this information to plan the content of future grammar lessons. For example, if many students in the class have difficulty with a Minute on commas, additional lessons in that area will be useful and valuable for the students' future success.

While Minute scores will not necessarily be included in students' formal grades, it is important to recognize student improvements by offering individual or class rewards and incentives for scores above a certain level on a daily and/or weekly basis. Showing students recognition for their efforts provides additional motivation to succeed.

Minute Journal

Name _____

Minute	Date	Score	Minute	Date	Score	Minute	Date	Score	Minute	Date	Score
1			26			51			76		
2			27			52			77		
3			28			53			78		
4			29			54			79		
5			30			55			80		
6			31			56			81		
7			32			57			82		
8			33			58			83		
9			34			59			84		
10			35			60			85		
11			36			61			86		
12			37			62			87		
13			38			63			88		
14			39			64			89		
15			40			65			90		
16			41			66			91		
17			42			67			92		
18			43			68			93		
19			44			69			94		
20			45			70			95		
21			46			71			96		
22			47			72			97		
23			48			73			98		
24			49			74			99		
25			50			75			100		

Grammar Minutes · Grade 1 © 2009 Creative Teaching Press

Scope and Sequence

Minute 1

Name _____

Put the words in the box in ABC order. Write the words on the lines.

| tap | rap | cap | map | zap | nap | lap | sap | gap | yap |

1. _____   6. _____

2. _____   7. _____

3. _____   8. _____

4. _____   9. _____

5. _____   10. _____

 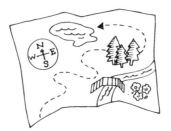 

Minute 2

Name _____

Put each set of words in ABC order.

gap   go   get

1. _____

2. _____

3. _____

can   cut   cop

4. _____

5. _____

6. _____

bed   bug   bat   bit

7. _____

8. _____

9. _____

10. _____

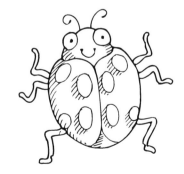

Grammar Minutes • Grade 1 © 2009 Creative Teaching Press

ABC Order Using the Second Letter

Minute 3

Name _____

Circle *Yes* if each set of words is in ABC order or *No* if it is not.

1.	at	mat	sat	Yes	No
2.	bad	sad	mad	Yes	No
3.	ant	ox	bug	Yes	No
4.	ball	cat	gas	Yes	No
5.	jam	run	sun	Yes	No
6.	sat	at	bat	Yes	No
7.	car	fox	ten	Yes	No
8.	top	dog	pan	Yes	No
9.	pen	pan	pot	Yes	No
10.	cap	cot	cut	Yes	No

Grammar Minutes • Grade 1 © 2009 Creative Teaching Press

Minute 4

Name _____

Choose the correct word to write at the beginning of each sentence.
Write it on the line.

1. _____ cat's name is Tabby.
      my   My

2. _____ am going to the park.
      I   i

3. _____ flower smells sweet.
      The   the

4. _____ cleans her room.
      Susan   susan

5. _____ likes the color purple.
      He   he

6. _____ are in the tree.
      birds   Birds

7. _____ is your mother?
      how   How

8. _____ eats a snack.
      she   She

9. _____ is not good for your teeth.
      Candy   candy

10. _____ can write his name.
      danny   Danny

Grammar Minutes · Grade 1 © 2009 Creative Teaching Press

Beginning a Sentence

Minute 5

Name _____

Choose the correct punctuation mark for the ending of each sentence. Write it on the line.
(**Hint**: A period (.) = a telling sentence; a question mark (?) = an asking sentence; and an exclamation point (!) = an exclaiming sentence.)

1. The dog is loud ____   .   ?   !

2. How are you ____   .   ?   !

3. Maria got a doll ____   .   ?   !

4. I won a bike ____   .   ?   !

5. Where is he ____   .   ?   !

6. Joe likes dogs ____   .   ?   !

7. Get off the desk ____   .   ?   !

8. I am at school ____   .   ?   !

9. Where is my book ____   .   ?   !

10. May I go now ____   .   ?   !

Grammar Minutes · Grade 1 © 2009 Creative Teaching Press

Minute 6

Name _____

Read each group of words. Circle *Complete* if each group of words is a complete sentence or *Not Complete* if it is not.

(**Hint**: A sentence tells a complete idea and has a naming part and a telling part.)

1. The dog is black.   Complete   Not Complete

2. The boy.   Complete   Not Complete

3. The water is cold.   Complete   Not Complete

4. Jumps on the bed.   Complete   Not Complete

5. My dad and I go fishing.   Complete   Not Complete

6. Jon likes comic books.   Complete   Not Complete

7. Running around the tree.   Complete   Not Complete

8. Madison bakes cookies.   Complete   Not Complete

9. The girl picks red flowers.   Complete   Not Complete

10. The zebra at the zoo.   Complete   Not Complete

Minute 7

Name _____

Read each pair of sentences. Circle the correct sentence in each pair.

1. a. The clouds are fluffy.
    b. Clouds are the fluffy.

2. a. Sky is dark the.
    b. The sky is dark.

3. a. The came down rain.
    b. The rain came down.

4. a. Need water my flowers.
    b. My flowers need water.

5. a. She plays in the rain.
    b. Plays in the rain she.

6. a. Rainbows I see like to.
    b. I like to see rainbows.

7. a. My reads mom a book.
    b. My mom reads a book.

8. a. We played board games.
    b. Games we played board.

9. a. Pete our dog scared was.
    b. Our dog Pete was scared.

10. a. It was a fun day.
    b. Was a fun day it.

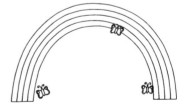

Grammar Minutes • Grade 1 © 2009 Creative Teaching Press

Minute 8

Name _____

Read each sentence and circle the type of sentence it is. Circle *T* for telling, *A* for asking, or *E* for exclaiming.

1.	The apples on the tree are red.	T	A	E
2.	Can we please have pizza?	T	A	E
3.	Where is the party?	T	A	E
4.	That is great news!	T	A	E
5.	I like reptiles.	T	A	E
6.	Sit down now!	T	A	E
7.	The policeman was nice.	T	A	E
8.	Are we going to the zoo?	T	A	E
9.	I broke the jar!	T	A	E
10.	I am six years old.	T	A	E

Types of Sentences

Minute 9

Name _____

Circle the naming part in each sentence.
(**Hint**: The naming part of a sentence tells who or what the sentence is about.)

1. The circus was fun.

The circus   was fun.

2. Tori and Cindy are twins.

Tori and Cindy   are twins.

3. My mother is the best cook.

My mother   is the best cook.

4. John wants a sandwich.

John   wants a sandwich.

5. The boy waits for his turn.

The boy   waits for his turn.

6. Spiders scare the little girl.

Spiders   scare the little girl.

7. The clouds are fluffy.

The clouds   are fluffy.

8. Mackenzie and Kayln are friends.

Mackenzie and Kayln   are friends.

9. I like to watch television.

I   like to watch television.

10. The birds are hungry.

The birds   are hungry.

Grammar Minutes • Grade 1 © 2009 Creative Teaching Press

Minute 10

Name _____

Circle the telling part in each sentence.
(**Hint**: The telling part of a sentence tells what someone or something does.)

1. My family works in the yard.
   My family   works in the yard.

2. My brother rakes the leaves.
   My brother   rakes the leaves.

3. My mother watches us play.
   My mother   watches us play.

4. I jump into the leaves.
   I   jump into the leaves.

5. Our dog chases me.
   Our dog   chases me.

6. My sister picks up trash.
   My sister   picks up trash.

7. My father mows the grass.
   My father   mows the grass.

8. My mother makes lunch.
   My mother   makes lunch.

9. We eat when we are done.
   We   eat when we are done.

10. The yard looks nice.
    The yard   looks nice.

Grammar Minutes · Grade 1 © 2009 Creative Teaching Press

Telling Parts of Sentences

Minute 11

Name _____

Put the words in the box in ABC order. Write the words on the lines.

| ox   bug   cat   fish   pig   fox   duck   ant   bird   dog |

1. _____

2. _____

3. _____

4. _____

5. _____

6. _____

7. _____

8. _____

9. _____

10. _____

Grammar Minutes • Grade 1 © 2009 Creative Teaching Press

Minute 12

Name _____

For Numbers 1–5, read each pair of sentences. Circle the correct sentence in each pair.

1. **a.** Meg likes ice cream.
b. meg likes ice cream.

2. **a.** i gave my dog a bath.
b. I gave my dog a bath.

3. **a.** Bobby plays at school.
b. bobby plays at school.

4. **a.** Mason beats on his drum.
b. mason beats on his drum.

5. **a.** brandon likes oranges.
b. Brandon likes oranges.

For Numbers 6–10, circle the correct punctuation mark for the ending of each sentence. Write it on the line.

6. Watch out for the snake _____ . ? !

7. I do not like snakes _____ . ? !

8. Do you like snakes _____ . ? !

9. My brother thinks snakes are cool _____ . ? !

10. May we look at another animal _____ . ? !

Beginning and Ending a Sentence Review

Minute 13

Name _____

For Numbers 1–4, circle *Complete* if each group of words is a complete sentence or *Not Complete* if it is not.

1. Feeds the cat.   Complete   Not Complete

2. Cary loves to paint.   Complete   Not Complete

3. Josh catches the ball.   Complete   Not Complete

4. Cleaning my room.   Complete   Not Complete

For Numbers 5–7, rewrite the sentences in the correct word order.

5. kitten my white is.   _____

6. to read like I stories.   _____

7. teacher is our funny.   _____

For Numbers 8–10, read each sentence and circle the type of sentence it is. Circle *T* for telling, *A* for asking, or *E* for exclaiming.

8. Are you happy?   T   A   E

9. I am excited about my birthday!   T   A   E

10. My parents are very nice.   T   A   E

Grammar Minutes • Grade 1 © 2009 Creative Teaching Press

Minute 14

Name _____

For Numbers 1–5, circle the naming part in each sentence.
(**Hint**: Remember that the naming part of a sentence tells who or what the sentence is about.)

1. Chris has piano practice.
Chris   has piano practice.

2. The candle is hot.
The candle   is hot.

3. The bat hangs upside down.
The bat   hangs upside down.

4. My parents are happy.
My parents   are happy.

5. Mr. Paul gave a test.
Mr. Paul   gave a test.

For Numbers 6–10, circle the telling part in each sentence.
(**Hint**: Remember that the telling part of a sentence tells what someone or something does.)

6. My dog chases the cat.
My dog   chases the cat.

7. The rabbit hops away.
The rabbit   hops away.

8. The butterfly sits on the flower.
The butterfly   sits on the flower.

9. The man tells funny stories.
The man   tells funny stories.

10. My frog Ribbit jumps up.
My frog Ribbit   jumps up.

Naming and Telling Parts of Sentences Review

Minute 15

Name _____

Circle the naming word for a person in each sentence.
(**Hint**: Each sentence only has one naming word, or noun, for a person.)

1. Nia likes to read.

Nia   likes   to   read.

2. The baby is little.

The   baby   is   little.

3. My teacher is pretty.

My   teacher   is   pretty.

4. Ryan plays games.

Ryan   plays   games.

5. The woman drives fast.

The   woman   drives   fast.

6. My mother cooks dinner.

My   mother   cooks   dinner.

7. Sarah bakes cookies.

Sarah   bakes   cookies.

8. The mailman brings letters.

The   mailman   brings   letters.

9. The zookeeper loves her job.

The   zookeeper   loves   her   job.

10. Shawn says hello.

Shawn   says   hello.

Grammar Minutes • Grade 1 © 2009 Creative Teaching Press

Minute 16

Name _____

Circle the naming word for a place in each sentence.
(**Hint:** Each sentence only has one naming word, or noun, for a place.)

1. Our school is big.

Our   school   is   big.

2. The classroom has windows.

The   classroom   has   windows.

3. The library has many books.

The   library   has   many   books.

4. We eat lunch in the cafeteria.

We   eat   lunch   in   the   cafeteria.

5. The bathroom is clean.

The   bathroom   is   clean.

6. We play games outside.

We   play   games   outside.

7. I skip on the playground.

I   skip   on   the   playground.

8. The nurse has an office.

The   nurse   has   an   office.

9. We walk across the yard.

We   walk   across   the   yard.

10. We shop at that store.

We   shop   at   that   store.

Grammar Minutes · Grade 1 © 2009 Creative Teaching Press

Minute 17

Name _____

Circle the naming word for a thing in each sentence.
(**Hint**: Each sentence only has one naming word, or noun, for a thing.)

1. The children use crayons to draw.

The children use crayons to draw.

2. That story was too scary!

That story was too scary!

3. Hang up your coat.

Hang up your coat.

4. Ashley drinks milk every day.

Ashley drinks milk every day.

5. Take out your scissors.

Take out your scissors.

6. The clock is round.

The clock is round.

7. Where is your homework?

Where is your homework?

8. Alex puts his money away.

Alex puts his money away.

9. This dress is my favorite.

This dress is my favorite.

10. I write on the paper.

I write on the paper.

Grammar Minutes • Grade 1 © 2009 Creative Teaching Press

Minute 18

Name _____

For Numbers 1–5, circle the naming word for an animal in each sentence.

1. The birds are yellow.

The   birds   are   yellow.

2. This is my sister's cat.

This   is   my   sister's   cat.

3. The otter swims in the river.

The   otter   swims   in   the   river.

4. My dog runs and plays.

My   dog   runs   and   plays.

5. We saw monkeys at the zoo.

We   saw   monkeys   at   the   zoo.

For Numbers 6–10, read each set of words. Circle the naming word for an animal in each set.

6. farmer   grass   cow   barn

7. ocean   shark   water   boat

8. zoo   cage   zookeeper   lion

9. doghouse   puppy   bone   bowl

10. desert   sand   camel   hot

Naming Words for Animals

Minute 19

Name _____

For Numbers 1–5, read each set of words. Circle the correct way to write the proper name for a person in each set.
(**Hint**: Proper names, or proper nouns, name special places, people, titles, and animals.)

1. ms. watson   Ms. watson   Ms. Watson

2. debra hill   Debra Hill   debra Hill

3. dr. young   dr. Young   Dr. Young

4. Uncle Max   uncle Max   uncle max

5. principal jones   Principal Jones   principal Jones

For Numbers 6–10, rewrite each proper name for a person correctly on the line.

6. mike james _____

7. coach jenkins _____

8. mrs. patrick _____

9. aunt meg _____

10. grandpa joe _____

Grammar Minutes • Grade 1 © 2009 Creative Teaching Press

Minute 20

Name _____

For Numbers 1–5, circle the proper name for a place in each sentence.
(**Hint**: Each proper name, or proper noun, has two words in it.)

1. My family went to Stone Park.

2. We live on Douglas Street.

3. I go to Simmons School.

4. May we go to Burger Hut for lunch?

5. Mike shops at Candy Mall.

For Numbers 6–10, rewrite each proper name for a place correctly on the line.

6. texas _____

7. new york _____

8. martin airport _____

9. flower trail _____

10. disneyland _____

Grammar Minutes · Grade 1 © 2009 Creative Teaching Press

Proper Names for Places

Minute 21

Name _____

Circle the proper name for an animal in each sentence.

1. We saw Ming the panda.

2. My cat Oscar is five years old.

3. Our class hamster is named Roxy.

4. Kate's favorite whale is Shimmer.

5. His snake Venom is huge.

6. May we take our puppy Duke with us?

7. Her rabbit Fluffy is white and black.

8. My dog Muffin is scared of noises.

9. We call our goldfish Simon.

10. The puppy's name will be Nella.

Grammar Minutes · Grade 1 © 2009 Creative Teaching Press

Minute 22

Name _____

Circle the proper name in each sentence that should begin with a capital letter. Write it correctly on the line.
(**Hint**: These proper names are for days, months, and holidays. Each sentence has one proper name that should begin with a capital letter.)

1. We play on saturday. _____

2. My birthday is in june. _____

3. Candace likes easter the best. _____

4. We see fireworks on the Fourth of july. _____

5. We go back to school in september. _____

6. The party is this friday. _____

7. My favorite holiday is valentine's Day. _____

8. Today is october 9, 2009. _____

9. Bill goes to the beach on tuesday. _____

10. She was born on april 16, 1988. _____

Other Proper Names (Days, Months, Holidays)

Minute 23

Name _____

For Numbers 1–5, write in the comma that is missing in each date.
(**Hint**: A comma belongs between the day and the year.)

1. May 28 2006

2. February 12 1996

3. April 16 1980

4. November 1 2008

5. June 15 2009

For Numbers 6–10, circle *Yes* if the commas in the dates are correct or *No* if they are not.

6. Sam will sing on May, 23, 2005.   Yes   No

7. I went there on October 31, 2007.   Yes   No

8. Today is June, 4 2008.   Yes   No

9. Kim cut her lip on January 1, 2008.   Yes   No

10. My grandma came on July 4, 2009.   Yes   No

Grammar Minutes · Grade 1 © 2009 Creative Teaching Press

Minute 24

Name _____

For Numbers 1–5, write in the comma that is missing in each sentence.
(**Hint**: A comma belongs between the name of a city and its state.)

1. Pat is from Madison Wisconsin.

2. Kelly was in Columbus Ohio.

3. Tracy lives in Selma Alabama.

4. We will stop at Houston Texas.

5. Where is San Francisco California?

For Numbers 6–10, circle the correct way to write the name of each place.
(**Hint**: The names of cities and states are proper names, and must begin with capital letters.)

6. Seattle washington   Seattle, Washington

7. Atlanta, Georgia   atlanta, georgia

8. miami, Florida   Miami, Florida

9. San Diego, California   San diego, California

10. New York, New York   New York, New york

Commas (places)

Minute 25

Name _____

Circle the naming words, or nouns, in the sentences.
(**Hint**: Remember that a noun can name a person, place, thing, or animal. Each sentence has two nouns.)

1. Apples and bananas taste good.

2. The girl has two sisters.

3. The students walk to the playground.

4. My friend rides her bike fast.

5. Our class is at the library.

6. The desks and chairs are wet.

7. The cat sleeps on the rug.

8. The flowers are in the garden.

9. The flashlight shines in the room.

10. There was food at the party.

Grammar Minutes · Grade 1 © 2009 Creative Teaching Press

Minute 26

Name _____

Each word in bold is a noun. Circle what each noun names.

1.	car	Person	Place	Thing	Animal
2.	school	Person	Place	Thing	Animal
3.	mom	Person	Place	Thing	Animal
4.	home	Person	Place	Thing	Animal
5.	cat	Person	Place	Thing	Animal
6.	student	Person	Place	Thing	Animal
7.	dish	Person	Place	Thing	Animal
8.	bird	Person	Place	Thing	Animal
9.	doctor	Person	Place	Thing	Animal
10.	fox	Person	Place	Thing	Animal

Grammar Minutes · Grade 1 © 2009 Creative Teaching Press

More Naming Words Review

Minute 27

Name _____

Circle the proper name in each sentence that is missing a capital letter. Rewrite it correctly on the line.

1. Greg is from virginia. _____

2. Amy and john go to school. _____

3. Ed's birthday is in february. _____

4. Lucy reads on saturday. _____

5. I got candy on halloween. _____

6. maria rides her bike. _____

7. Dr. carter helps me. _____

8. choco the cat is my pet. _____

9. School is closed on monday. _____

10. We shop at newport Mall. _____

Minute 28

Name _____

For Numbers 1–5, write in the missing comma in the date in each sentence.

1. Her birthday is on April 2 2009.

2. We will go on March 15 2008.

3. My party is on June 1 2010.

4. We saw him on December 20 2006.

5. The test is on September 30 2009.

For Numbers 6–10, write in the missing comma in the name of each place.

6. Hollywood California

7. Portland Oregon

8. Tucson Arizona

9. Denver Colorado

10. Chicago Illinois

Commas Review

Minute 29

Name _____

Circle the action word in each sentence.

(**Hint**: Action words, or verbs, tell what someone or something does. Each sentence has one action word.)

1. Bobbi sings in the play.

2. Stacey reads a letter.

3. Tony and Carl play tennis.

4. The students say hi to me.

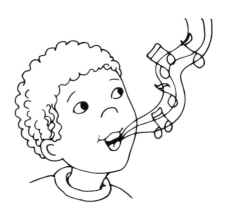

5. The plant grows fast.

6. I give letters to my friends.

7. The kids swim in the lake.

8. The sun rises in the east.

9. Dorothy skips on the rug.

10. Meg picks a flower.

Grammar Minutes • Grade 1 © 2009 Creative Teaching Press

Minute 30

Name _____

For Numbers 1–5, use an action word from the box to complete each sentence. Use each word only one time.

1. My sister and I _____ with our hands.

2. I _____ my mom and dad.

3. The leaves _____ from the tree.

4. I _____ him with his homework.

5. The frog _____ on the log.

fall
help
love
jumps
clap

For Numbers 6–10, circle the correct action word to complete each sentence.

6. The birds _____ high in the sky.
 fly   jump

7. They _____ at the table.
 eat   sleep

8. The wind _____ the leaves.
 likes   blows

9. We _____ chocolate cookies.
 make   sing

10. We can't _____ in the library.
 read   run

More on Action Words

Minute 31

Name _____

Choose the correct action word to complete each sentence. Write it on the line.

(**Hint**: Each sentence tells about something that happens now.)

1. The little boy _____ his dog.
      pets   pet

2. My mother _____ carrots.
      chop   chops

3. The baker _____ lots of cakes.
      bake   bakes

4. Pablo _____ lots of pictures.
      paints   paint

5. The big cat _____ the mouse.
      chase   chases

6. Sam _____ in the sand.
      plays   play

7. Carly _____ a castle.
      make   makes

8. The mouse _____ up the tree.
      runs   run

9. The tiger _____ its paws.
      licks   lick

10. My dog _____ at the cars.
       bark   barks

Grammar Minutes · Grade 1 © 2009 Creative Teaching Press

Minute 32

Name _____

For Numbers 1–5, use an action word from the box to complete each sentence. Use each word only one time.
(**Hint**: Each sentence tells about something that happened in the past. Many action words add **-ed** to show that something happened in the past.)

1. The puppy _____ with his toy.

2. The rose _____ sweet.

3. He _____ his tooth out.

4. I _____ the movie yesterday.

5. Lea _____ onto the bed.

pulled
watched
jumped
smelled
played

For Numbers 6–10, use an action word from the box to complete each sentence. Use each word only one time.

6. We _____ hot dogs and corn.

7. I _____ a question.

8. She _____ for the answer.

9. I _____ my hamster Harry.

10. My mom _____ the wall red.

painted
looked
asked
named
cooked

Past Tense Action Words

Minute 33

Name _____

Write the correct verb (*is, are,* or *am*) to complete each sentence.

1. I _____ happy to be here.
<u>is   are   am</u>

2. _____ we the winners?
<u>Is   Are   Am</u>

3. The big race _____ today.
<u>is   are   am</u>

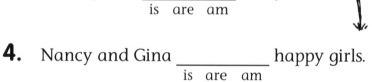

4. Nancy and Gina _____ happy girls.
<u>is   are   am</u>

5. They _____ home now.
<u>is   are   am</u>

6. I _____ in the school play.
<u>is   are   am</u>

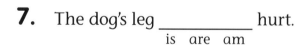

7. The dog's leg _____ hurt.
<u>is   are   am</u>

8. We _____ a good class.
<u>is   are   am</u>

9. Apples _____ my favorite fruit.
<u>is   are   am</u>

10. The weather _____ cold today.
<u>is   are   am</u>

Grammar Minutes · Grade 1 © 2009 Creative Teaching Press

Minute 34

Name _____

Write the correct verb (*was* or *were*) to complete each sentence.

1. I _____ with my friends.
   <u>was   were</u>

2. Four ducks _____ in the pond.
   <u>was   were</u>

3. The jar _____ on the table.
   <u>was   were</u>

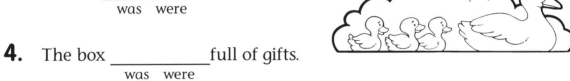

4. The box _____ full of gifts.
   <u>was   were</u>

5. The tigers _____ under the tree.
   <u>was   were</u>

6. His boat _____ blue and green.
   <u>was   were</u>

7. Tom and Jerry _____ cold in the snow.
   <u>was   were</u>

8. Last year she _____ not tall.
   <u>was   were</u>

9. The stars _____ pretty in the sky.
   <u>was   were</u>

10. My hair _____ cut yesterday.
   <u>was   were</u>

Grammar Minutes • Grade 1 © 2009 Creative Teaching Press

Linking Verbs (was, were)

Minute 35

Name _____

Circle *Yes* if the correct verb *(have, has,* or *had)* is used or *No* if it is not.

1. I <u>has</u> no more cookies.　　　　　　Yes　　　No

2. Erin <u>had</u> a hat on yesterday.　　　Yes　　　No

3. The birds <u>have</u> a worm to eat.　　Yes　　　No

4. They <u>have</u> a soccer game today.　Yes　　　No

5. The puppy <u>have</u> big paws.　　　　Yes　　　No

6. Last week he <u>has</u> two tests.　　　Yes　　　No

7. Bob <u>has</u> a sore throat last night.　Yes　　　No

8. The baby <u>has</u> one tooth.　　　　　Yes　　　No

9. The cat <u>has</u> a lot of fur.　　　　　Yes　　　No

10. I <u>have</u> two pink dresses.　　　　Yes　　　No

Grammar Minutes · Grade 1 © 2009 Creative Teaching Press

Minute 36

Name _____

For Numbers 1–5, read each pair of words. Circle the correct naming word that names more than one.

1. car   cars

2. song   songs

3. beds   bed

4. pets   pet

5. plane   planes

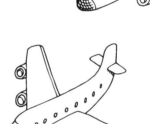

For Numbers 6–10, write each naming word to show more than one.

6. street   _____

7. bug   _____

8. book   _____

9. game   _____

10. tree   _____

Plural Naming Words (-s)

Minute 37

Name _____

For Numbers 1–6, read each pair of words. Circle the correct naming word that names more than one.

1. fox   foxes

2. dishes   dish

3. couch   couches

4. bush   bushes

5. glasses   glass

6. bus   buses

For Numbers 7–10, circle the naming word that names more than one in each sentence.

7. Sam has three watches.

8. These boxes are light.

9. The beaches in Florida are big.

10. Four classes went on the field trip.

Grammar Minutes · Grade 1 © 2009 Creative Teaching Press

Minute 38

Name _____

For Numbers 1–5, read each set of words. Circle the correct naming word that names more than one in each set.

1. hills   hilles   hill

2. peaches   peach   peachs

3. circus   circuses   circuss

4. spoons   spoon   spoones

5. wishes   wishs   wish

For Numbers 6–10, rewrite each naming word to show more than one.

6. hand   _____

7. ax   _____

8. coin   _____

9. branch   _____

10. bird   _____

More Plural Naming Words (-s, -es)

Minute 39

Name _____

Circle the action word in each sentence.

1. We eat hot dogs for lunch.

2. I pet my dog on the head.

3. My dad paints the house.

4. We ran in the race.

5. The tree grew tall.

6. I went to the store.

7. The ice melted in the sun.

8. We go to that park.

9. The band walked on the field.

10. My mom takes me to the park.

Grammar Minutes · Grade 1 © 2009 Creative Teaching Press

Minute 40

Name _____

Circle whether each sentence is in the *Present* or in the *Past*.
(**Hint**: When something happens now, it is *present*. When something happened already, it is *past*.)

1.	They fished in the lake yesterday.	Present	Past
2.	Susan listens to the teacher.	Present	Past
3.	I know all about whales.	Present	Past
4.	Regina helped her mom clean.	Present	Past
5.	Simon runs faster than everyone.	Present	Past
6.	Our kitten likes fresh milk.	Present	Past
7.	I kicked the ball in the air.	Present	Past
8.	We called Grandma Rose last night.	Present	Past
9.	The students ride on a bus.	Present	Past
10.	Joey wanted a bike last Christmas.	Present	Past

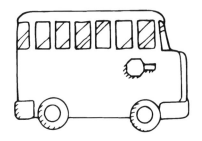

Present and Past Tense Review

Minute 41

Name _____

For Questions 1–5, use a verb from the box to complete each sentence. Use each word only one time.

1. Lisa _____ two eggs for breakfast.

2. We _____ with my dad yesterday.

3. Joey _____ in music class now.

4. I _____ seven years old today.

5. Why _____ you mad at me?

is

are

am

were

had

For Questions 6–10, write the correct verb to complete each sentence.

6. Where _____ my coat?
<u>is   are</u>

7. We _____ a party last Halloween.
<u>had   has</u>

8. Do you _____ a pen for me?
<u>has   have</u>

9. The wind _____ cold last night.
<u>were   was</u>

10. Molly _____ two best friends.
<u>have   has</u>

Minute 42

Name _____

For Numbers 1–5, read each pair of words. Circle the correct noun that names more than one.

1. cows   cowes

2. cupes   cups

3. witches   witchs

4. pailes   pails

5. foxes   foxs

For Numbers 6–10, write the correct noun to complete each sentence.

6. Her brother has five red _____.

hates   hats

7. They have two baby_____.

girls   girl

8. Our new _____ are very nice.

dishes   dish

9. These _____ sell toys.

store   stores

10. I made three _____ for my birthday.

wishs   wishes

Plural Naming Words Review

Minute 43

Name _____

Write *I* or *me* to complete each sentence.
(**Hint**: *I* is used in the naming part of a sentence, and *me* is used in the telling part of a sentence.)

1. _____ am a fast runner.

2. My mom gives _____ a snack every day.

3. Will you take _____ to the store?

4. _____ am very sleepy.

5. My baby sister loves _____.

6. Am _____ going with you?

7. He told _____ a funny story.

8. _____ am not cold.

9. Why am _____ so tall?

10. My friend Jen wrote _____ a letter.

Grammar Minutes • Grade 1 © 2009 Creative Teaching Press

Minute 44

Name _____

For Numbers 1–5, write *she* or *her* to complete each sentence.
(Hint: *She* and *her* take the place of a naming word for a girl or a woman. *She* is used in the naming part of a sentence, and *her* is used in the telling part of a sentence.)

1. I saw _____ eat the glue!

2. I want to give _____ flowers.

3. _____ is going to California.

4. Is _____ in bed yet?

5. I read my poem to _____ .

For Numbers 6–10, circle *she* or *her* to take the place of the underlined words.

6. <u>Anne</u> paints pretty pictures.
 She   Her

7. I made <u>my mom</u> a birthday card.
 she   her

8. <u>Our teacher</u> knows a lot of things.
 She   Her

9. Tom let <u>Lisa</u> use his pen.
 she   her

10. Do you like <u>the new girl in class</u>?
 she   her

Pronouns (she, her)

Minute 45

Name _____

For Numbers 1–5, circle *he* or *him* to take the place of the underlined words.
(**Hint**: *He* and *him* take the place of a naming word for a boy or a man. *He* is used in the naming part of a sentence, and *him* is used in the telling part of a sentence.)

1. <u>The man</u> sleeps on the couch.

He   Him

2. <u>Harry</u> likes to play in the snow.

He   Him

3. I can ride my bike faster than <u>Phil</u>.

he   him

4. The teacher is looking at <u>Jack</u>.

he   him

5. <u>The policeman</u> helps people.

He   Him

For Numbers 6–10, read the first sentence, and then write *he* or *him* to complete the second sentence.

6. My dad works at a school. _____ is a teacher.

7. I saw John yesterday. I played cars with _____.

8. His brother plays football. _____ is strong!

9. That man eats a lot. _____ is always hungry.

10. Matt is in my class. I sit near _____.

Grammar Minutes · Grade 1 © 2009 Creative Teaching Press

Minute 46

Name _____

For Numbers 1–5, circle *they* or *them* to take the place of the underlined words.
(**Hint:** *They* is used in the naming part of a sentence, and *them* is used in the telling part of a sentence.)

1.	<u>Her gifts</u> are on the desk.	They	Them
2.	<u>The girls</u> like to paint their nails.	They	Them
3.	We saw <u>his mom and dad</u> outside.	they	them
4.	<u>Luke and Tim</u> are going to Disney World.	They	Them
5.	Susie says hello to <u>her friends</u>.	they	them

For Numbers 6–10, write *they* or *them* to take the place of the underlined words.

6. Mrs. Hill tells <u>the boys</u> to stop. _____

7. <u>My grandparents</u> are coming to visit. _____

8. <u>The birds</u> are in the nest. _____

9. Pam has <u>her toys</u> at school. _____

10. <u>The girls</u> talk all day. _____

Pronouns (they, them)

Minute 47

Name _____

For Numbers 1–5, write *we* or *us* to complete each sentence.
(**Hint**: *We* is used in the naming part of a sentence, and *us* is used in the telling part of a sentence.)

1. _____ have a cat and a dog.
   <u>We   Us</u>

2. Why does he yell at _____?
   <u>we   us</u>

3. They are taking _____ to the zoo.
   <u>we   us</u>

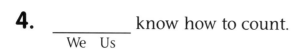

4. _____ know how to count.
   <u>We   Us</u>

5. My mom was with _____.
   <u>we   us</u>

For Numbers 6–10, circle *Yes* if the underlined pronoun is used correctly or *No* if it is not.

6. <u>Us</u> take a bath at night.   Yes   No

7. <u>We</u> write thank-you letters.   Yes   No

8. The teacher tells <u>we</u> a story.   Yes   No

9. Why are <u>us</u> going there?   Yes   No

10. The dog licked <u>us</u> on the face.   Yes   No

Grammar Minutes · Grade 1 © 2009 Creative Teaching Press

Minute 48

Name _____

For Numbers 1–5, write the correct describing word to complete each sentence.
(Hint: These describing words, or adjectives, tell about size.)

1. The _____ baby cried for his mother.
old   little

2. The _____ tree was cut down.
tall   ugly

3. I like the elephant because it is _____.
big   light

4. The worm is very _____.
long   dirty

5. A _____ ant is on my arm.
black   small

For Numbers 6–10, circle the describing word in each sentence.
(Hint: These describing words, or adjectives, tell about shape.)

6. Sarah has a round pumpkin.

7. The square clock is on the wall.

8. The pancakes we made are flat.

9. My brother has an oval face.

10. These french fries are so skinny!

Grammar Minutes · Grade 1 © 2009 Creative Teaching Press

Describing Words (size and shape)

Minute 49

Name _____

Circle the describing word in each sentence.
(**Hint**: These describing words, or adjectives, tell about colors and numbers.)

1. Her dress was pink.

2. She wore two bows in her hair.

3. The blue bird flies away.

4. The four friends eat pizza.

5. My three children are boys.

6. We both like red apples.

7. The black dog is nice.

8. The yellow stars are in the sky.

9. Please take five pieces of candy.

10. The three boys went home.

Grammar Minutes • Grade 1 © 2009 Creative Teaching Press

Minute 50

Name _____

Circle the describing word in each sentence.
(**Hint**: These describing words, or adjectives, tell about taste and smell.)

1. The apple was sweet.

2. The lemon is sour.

3. I don't like spicy chips.

4. My bedroom smells clean.

5. This gum is minty.

6. Our dinner was yummy.

7. Grapes are a tasty treat.

8. Those eggs must be rotten!

9. I like to eat creamy soups.

10. My dog is so stinky!

Grammar Minutes · Grade 1 © 2009 Creative Teaching Press

Describing Words (taste and smell)

Minute 51

Name _____

Circle the describing word in each sentence.
(**Hint**: These describing words, or adjectives, tell about touch and sound.)

1. My soft cat is named Bella.

2. His loud snoring woke everyone up.

3. I like her fuzzy sweater.

4. The hard ball hit my head.

5. The squeaky door opened.

6. He loves the silky blanket.

7. The squealing pig ate corn.

8. The chirping birds sat in the tree.

9. The rough wood needs sanding.

10. The sharp knife cut him.

Grammar Minutes · Grade 1 © 2009 Creative Teaching Press

Minute 52

Name _____

For Numbers 1–5, write the describing word that completes each sentence.

(**Hint:** When describing words compare two things, they sometimes end in *-er*.)

1. Tyra is _____ than my brother.

                     tall   taller

2. I think math is _____ than science.

                     easy   easier

3. Their house is much _____ than our house.

                     bigger   big

4. It is _____ in August than it is in December.

                 hotter   hot

5. Our dog is _____ than our cat.

                   old   older

For Numbers 6–10, complete each sentence with the correct describing word.

(**Hint:** Use the underlined word in each sentence to help you figure out the missing word.)

6. My ruler is <u>long</u>, but the teacher's ruler is even _____.

7. Last winter was <u>cold</u>, but this winter is much _____.

8. I can run <u>fast</u>, but not _____ than my friend Luke.

9. Patty is <u>nice</u> to me, but her sister is even _____ to me.

10. A bird flies <u>high</u>, but an airplane can go _____.

Minute 53

Name _____

For Numbers 1–5, write the describing word that completes each sentence.

(**Hint**: When describing words compare more than two things, they sometimes end in **-est**.)

1. Kelly is the _____ person in our class.
stronger   strongest

2. Our dog was the _____ dog at the dog park.
small   smallest

3. My grandpa has one of the _____ coins in the world.
oldest   older

4. We all tell funny jokes, but Jim tells the _____ jokes of all.
funniest   funny

5. A writer in Germany wrote the _____ sentence ever.
long   longest

For Numbers 6–10, write *Yes* if the underlined describing word is correct or *No* if it is not.

6. Nelson has the <u>small</u> pencil I have ever seen.   _____

7. Lisa is the <u>smartest</u> person I know.   _____

8. Bart made the <u>bigger</u> mess of all.   _____

9. I read the <u>longest</u> book in the library.   _____

10. Our teacher is the <u>nicest</u> one in the school.   _____

Grammar Minutes • Grade 1 © 2009 Creative Teaching Press

Minute 54

Name _____

Circle *Yes* if the underlined pronoun in each sentence is correct or *No* if it is not.

1. <u>Him</u> has a tennis game today.   Yes   No

2. <u>I</u> always wash the dishes for my mom.   Yes   No

3. Give Don's pencil back to <u>he</u>.   Yes   No

4. Santa gave <u>me</u> a new bike last year.   Yes   No

5. We are asking <u>they</u> to come over.   Yes   No

6. Please help <u>us</u> find the lost kitten.   Yes   No

7. Where are <u>them</u> going?   Yes   No

8. I told my grandma I would call <u>her</u> later.   Yes   No

9. Michael and <u>me</u> go camping all the time.   Yes   No

10. <u>Them</u> are going skating this Sunday.   Yes   No

Pronouns Review

Minute 55

Name _____

For Numbers 1–5, circle the correct pronoun to take the place of the underlined words.

1. Katie walked her dog to the park.

    She   Her

2. I gave Nancy and Liz some of my stickers.

    they   them

3. We saw the clown at the circus.

    he   him

4. My brother got my mom and me sick.

    we   us

5. Jeff said I hit Jenny, but I didn't.

    she   her

For Numbers 6–10, read the first sentence, and then write the correct pronoun missing in the second sentence.

6. Jerry is so smart. _____ always gets good grades.

                      He Him

7. The Cruz sisters can sing. _____ can also dance.

                      They Them

8. I asked my parents for a pony. They told _____ "no."

                      I me

9. Dr. Smith is nice. We went to see _____ yesterday.

                      he him

10. Mrs. Potter likes my sister. She gave _____ a book.

                      she her

Grammar Minutes • Grade 1 © 2009 Creative Teaching Press

Minute 56

Name _____

Circle the describing words in the sentences.
(**Hint**: Each sentence has two describing words, or adjectives, to circle.)

1. The tall man ate the spicy chicken.

2. Tommy is wearing dark pants and big boots.

3. There are red apples in the white basket.

4. The sweet juice is in a tall glass.

5. Kim's warm jacket is furry.

6. The black banana is rotten.

7. I had one penny and two dimes.

8. The square pillow is soft.

9. Lou made a dark chocolate cake.

10. The loud dog barked at the quiet cat.

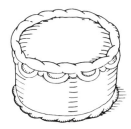

Grammar Minutes · Grade 1 © 2009 Creative Teaching Press

Describing Words Review

Minute 57

Name _____

For Numbers 1–5, write the describing word that completes each sentence.

1. My hair is _____ than my sister's hair.
<u>longer   longest</u>

2. Our tree is the _____ one on the street.
<u>taller   tallest</u>

3. Wendy got to school _____ than anyone.
<u>later   latest</u>

4. That black kitten is the _____ of them all.
<u>cuter   cutest</u>

5. I have the _____ desk in the class.
<u>cleaner   cleanest</u>

For Numbers 6–10, read each set of sentences. Write the correct describing word missing in each set.

6. I am tall. He is _____. She is the tallest of all.

7. A cat is small. A mouse is smaller. An ant is the _____ of all.

8. Apples are sweet. Soda is _____. Candy is the sweetest of all.

9. He is nice. She is _____. I am the nicest of all.

10. The music is loud. That music is louder. This music is the _____.

Minute 58

Name _____

Circle the noun in each sentence that shows ownership.
(**Hint**: An apostrophe and an *s* ('s) on naming words, or nouns, show ownership.)

1. Sally's dog is dirty.

2. The plane's wings are white.

3. The cat's ball of yarn is purple.

4. Dean's bike needs a new tire.

5. Maria's favorite color is pink.

6. The tree's leaves are yellow.

7. The park's slide is very long.

8. The computer's mouse is lost.

9. The bunny's ears are furry.

10. Becky's family is going to Tampa.

Nouns That Show Ownership ('s)

Minute 59

Name _____

For Numbers 1–5, write *Yes* if the underlined noun shows ownership or *No* if it does not.

1. The <u>bird's</u> feathers were blue.   _____

2. My new <u>doll</u> is very tall.   _____

3. The <u>tree's</u> branches are thick.   _____

4. <u>Robert's</u> coat keeps him warm.   _____

5. The <u>clock</u> rang loudly.   _____

For Numbers 6–10, draw a line to match each group of words on the left with the correct way to show ownership on the right.

6. fur on the cat   **a.** shirt's button

7. car that belongs to the man   **b.** woman's hat

8. button on the shirt   **c.** cat's fur

9. toy that belongs to the girl   **d.** man's car

10. hat on the woman   **e.** girl's toy

Grammar Minutes · Grade 1 © 2009 Creative Teaching Press

Minute 60

Name _____

Write the correct verb to complete each sentence.

1. My mom _____ my bed.
     make   makes

2. The girl _____ in a pretty voice.
     sing   sings

3. The boy _____ too loudly.
     talk   talks

4. The dog will _____ his tail at his owner.
     wag   wags

5. Fred _____ his car.
     wash   washes

6. The birds _____ to their nest.
     fly   flies

7. Rachel _____ her keys all the time.
     lose   loses

8. Ken _____ his bike to work.
     ride   rides

9. The zebras _____ through the grass.
     run   runs

10. My dad _____ faster than my mom.
      drive   drives

Grammar Minutes · Grade 1 © 2009 Creative Teaching Press

Noun and Verb Agreement

Minute 61

Name _____

For Numbers 1–5, use the verbs in the box to complete each sentence. Use each word only one time.

1. The girls _____ each other goodbye.

2. The woman _____ on the track every day.

3. Charles _____ basketball on Mondays.

4. The children _____ lots of candy at this store.

5. Karla and Michelle _____ cookies to sell.

plays

buy

runs

bake

hug

For Numbers 6–10, write the correct verb to complete each sentence.

6. The baby _____ his food on the floor.
          throw   throws

7. Kate _____ bubbles with her gum.
          blow   blows

8. Patrick _____ along the path.
          skip   skips

9. Steve and John _____ books in the library.
          read   reads

10. The spiders _____ webs on the barn.
          make   makes

Grammar Minutes • Grade 1 © 2009 Creative Teaching Press

Minute 62

Name _____

Write the correct noun that names more than one in each sentence.
(**Hint**: These naming words, or nouns, change spelling to name more than one.)

1. Five _____ cried when they saw the clown.
  childs   children

2. I read a story about _____ who help a fairy princess.
  elfs   elves

3. All of the _____ ran into the hole.
  mice   mouses

4. The _____ swam slowly in the water.
  gooses   geese

5. The dentist took out two of my _____.
  teeth   toothes

6. All the _____ in my family are tall.
  womans   women

7. The _____ are playing with the kids outside.
  men   mans

8. Linda's _____ are bigger than my feet.
  feet   foots

9. Many _____ like to eat ice cream.
  peoples   people

10. The _____ on the tree turned yellow.
  leaves   leafs

Irregular Plural Nouns

Minute 63

Name _____

For Numbers 1–5, read each set of words. Circle the correct noun that names more than one in each set.

1. childs   children   childes

2. shelves   shelfes   shelfs

3. tooths   teeth   teeths

4. life   lifes   lives

5. feet   foots   footes

For Numbers 6–10, rewrite each noun to show more than one.

6. man   _____

7. wolf   _____

8. woman   _____

9. goose   _____

10. mouse   _____

Grammar Minutes • Grade 1 © 2009 Creative Teaching Press

Minute 64

Name _____

Write the correct verb to complete each sentence.

1. I _____ the horses at the ranch.
    <u>saw</u>   <u>seen</u>

2. Kelly _____ the party early.
    <u>leaved</u>   <u>left</u>

3. Tom _____ the ducks at the pond.
    <u>feed</u>   <u>fed</u>

4. I _____ a tooth during lunch.
    <u>lost</u>   <u>lose</u>

5. Sherry was so thirsty she _____ all the water.
    <u>drinked</u>   <u>drank</u>

6. The story Kris _____ won a prize.
    <u>wrote</u>   <u>write</u>

7. Roxy and Bianca _____ lunch with their dad.
    <u>ate</u>   <u>eated</u>

8. Darren _____ out of the tree this afternoon.
    <u>fell</u>   <u>fall</u>

9. Holly _____ in the deep end of the pool.
    <u>swam</u>   <u>swimmed</u>

10. My dad _____ slowly in the rain.
    <u>drove</u>   <u>drived</u>

Irregular Verbs

Minute 65

Name _____

For Numbers 1–5, circle the correct past-tense verb in each pair.

1. maked   made

2. wrote   writed

3. fell   falled

4. breaked   broke

5. took   taked

For Numbers 6–10, write each verb in the past tense.
(**Hint**: These are irregular verbs, which are verbs that do not add *-ed* to tell about the past.)

6. see _____

7. run _____

8. eat _____

9. come _____

10. say _____

Grammar Minutes • Grade 1 © 2009 Creative Teaching Press

Minute 66

Name _____

Write _a_ or _an_ in front of each noun (naming word).
(**Hint**: Use _a_ before words that begin with a consonant sound. Use _an_ before words that begin with a vowel sound. The vowels are _a, e, i, o,_ and _u._)

1. _____ apple

2. _____ computer

3. _____ glass

4. _____ igloo

5. _____ egg

6. _____ team

7. _____ cage

8. _____ ostrich

9. _____ umbrella

10. _____ table

Articles (a, an)

Minute 67

Name _____

Write *a*, *an*, or *the* to complete each sentence.
(**Hint**: Remember that sentences must begin with a capital letter.)

1. _____ horses are running around the track.

2. _____ alligator creeps along the swamp.

3. We are taking _____ airplane to New Mexico.

4. _____ barber on Jones Street cuts my hair.

5. _____ ladybug sits on the leaf.

6. Jackie rakes _____ leaves into a pile.

7. I can't find _____ pencil to use.

8. May I have _____ ice cream cone?

9. I had pancakes and _____ apple for breakfast.

10. _____ class is ready for the field trip.

Grammar Minutes • Grade 1 © 2009 Creative Teaching Press

Minute 68

Name _____

For Numbers 1–5, circle the noun in each sentence that shows ownership.

1. Maggie's writing is not very messy.

2. Carrie's blanket is soft and warm.

3. The girl's tooth fell out this morning.

4. Bob's math homework is all correct.

5. Our dog's puppies were born last night.

For Numbers 6–10, write *Yes* if the underlined noun shows ownership or *No* if it does not.

6. The <u>plant</u> leaves are bright green. _____

7. The <u>house's</u> gate is painted white. _____

8. <u>Carol's</u> grandmother is coming to visit. _____

9. The <u>firefighter</u> truck drove by. _____

10. The <u>baby's</u> bottle needs more milk. _____

Grammar Minutes · Grade 1 © 2009 Creative Teaching Press

Nouns That Show Ownership Review

Minute 69

Name _____

For Numbers 1–5, write the correct verb to complete each sentence.

1. Emily _____ three laps around the pool.
 swims   swim

2. Heidi _____ Emily swim.
 watch   watched

3. Kate and Lea _____ to swim too.
 like   likes

4. All of the girls _____ into the pool.
 dive   dives

5. They _____ each other in the pool.
 raced   races

For Numbers 6–10, use the verbs in the box to complete each sentence. Use each word only one time.

washed	rings	takes	does	wins

6. Lupita always _____ when we race.

7. The baby _____ a nap every afternoon.

8. My brother and I _____ the dishes last night.

9. The phone _____ a lot in our house.

10. The new student _____ the best work he can.

Grammar Minutes · Grade 1 © 2009 Creative Teaching Press

Minute 70

Name _____

For Numbers 1–5, circle whether each noun names *One* or *More than one.*

1. leaves   One   More than one

2. person   One   More than one

3. wolf   One   More than one

4. men   One   More than one

5. knives   One   More than one

For Numbers 6–10, circle whether each sentence describes something in the *Present* (happening now) or in the *Past* (already happened).

6. I bring my lunch to school.   Present   Past

7. My mom bought that book for me.   Present   Past

8. We all went camping last summer.   Present   Past

9. The movie star flies his own plane.   Present   Past

10. I felt sick after I ate that whole pie! Present   Past

Grammar Minutes · Grade 1 © 2009 Creative Teaching Press

Irregular Plural Nouns and Verbs Review

Minute 71

Name _____

Write *Yes* if the underlined article is correct or *No* if it is not.
(**Hint**: *A, an,* and *the* are called articles.)

1. <u>An</u> pear is my favorite fruit. _____

2. <u>The</u> shoes hurt my feet. _____

3. We go to <u>the</u> pond by my house to fish. _____

4. <u>A</u> car crashed into a tree. _____

5. Sue is excited about riding <u>an</u> elephant
at the circus. _____

6. <u>A</u> boots belong to my mother. _____

7. <u>An</u> octopus is swimming nearby. _____

8. I want to go to <u>an</u> summer camp. _____

9. The little girl eats <u>a</u> slice of cherry pie. _____

10. Please don't put <u>an</u> orange in my lunch. _____

Grammar Minutes · Grade 1 © 2009 Creative Teaching Press

Minute 72

Name _____

Circle the compound word in each sentence.
(**Hint**: A compound word is made up of two words. Each sentence has only one compound word to circle.)

1. I can't find my watch in my bedroom.

2. We have a pool in our backyard.

3. My shoelaces are too short for my shoes.

4. The sunshine felt warm on my skin.

5. We saw jellyfish at the beach.

6. My mother baked homemade bread.

7. Give your teacher your homework.

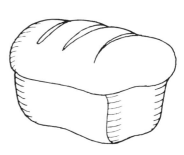

8. My uncle has three grandchildren.

9. I ate eggs and sausage for breakfast.

10. Ride your bike on the sidewalk.

Grammar Minutes · Grade 1 © 2009 Creative Teaching Press

Compound Words

Minute 73

Name _____

Write *Yes* if each word is a compound word or *No* if it is not.

1. songbird _____

2. grass _____

3. slide _____

4. highway _____

5. seashell _____

6. pencil _____

7. chalkboard _____

8. sailboat _____

9. radio _____

10. rainbow _____

Grammar Minutes • Grade 1 © 2009 Creative Teaching Press

Minute 74

Name _____

For Numbers 1–5, read each pair of words. Circle the correct contraction in each pair.

(**Hint**: A contraction is a word made when you join two words. But unlike compound words, a contraction uses an apostrophe (') to show where a letter or letters were left out.)

1. isn't   isnt'

2. hasnt   hasn't

3. don't   do'nt

4. ca'nt   can't

5. willn't   won't

For Numbers 6–10, use the contractions in the box to complete each sentence. Use each word only one time.

shouldn't	haven't	isn't	don't	won't

6. I _____ seen that movie yet.

7. The students _____ know how to add.

8. You _____ give the little dog a big bone.

9. Sarah _____ be seven years old until May.

10. My letter from Aunt Janet _____ here yet.

Grammar Minutes · Grade 1 © 2009 Creative Teaching Press

Contractions with not

Minute 75

Name _____

For Numbers 1–6, draw a line to match each group of words on the left with its correct contraction on the right.

1. I am   **a.** you're

2. it is   **b.** she's

3. you are   **c.** we're

4. they are   **d.** I'm

5. she is   **e.** it's

6. we are   **f.** they're

For Numbers 7–10, use the contractions in the box to complete each sentence. Use each word only one time.

> you're   I'm   we're   she's

7. We get in trouble when _____ too loud.

8. Estella, _____ the best friend I have.

9. Everyone tells Britney that _____ a good singer.

10. _____ getting my new bike today.

Grammar Minutes • Grade 1 © 2009 Creative Teaching Press

Minute 76

Name _____

For Numbers 1–5, circle the correct synonym that goes with each clue.
(**Hint**: A synonym is a word that means the same thing or almost the same thing.)

1. This word means the same as <u>glad</u>.
   happy   sad

2. This word means the same as <u>big</u>.
   little   large

3. This word means the same as <u>beautiful</u>.
   pretty   ugly

4. This word means the same as <u>fast</u>.
   slow   quick

5. This word means the same as <u>yell</u>.
   shout   whisper

For Numbers 6–10, draw a line to match the underlined word in each sentence on the left with its correct synonym on the right.

6. All of her answers were <u>correct</u>.   **a.** mad

7. The clown told us <u>funny</u> jokes.   **b.** start

8. The <u>tiny</u> mouse ran through the hole.   **c.** right

9. We will <u>begin</u> the test in five minutes.   **d.** small

10. My mother was <u>angry</u> with me.   **e.** silly

Grammar Minutes · Grade 1 © 2009 Creative Teaching Press

Synonyms

Minute 77

Name _____

For Numbers 1–6, read each set of words. Circle the two synonyms in each set.

1. hot   warm   cold

2. see   say   look

3. fat   thin   thick

4. sleep   nap   awake

5. kind   mean   nice

6. close   open   shut

For Numbers 7–10, read each pair of sentences. Look at the underlined word in the first sentence. Circle its synonym in the second sentence.

7. Our new television is <u>large</u>. It is too big for the room.

8. The rabbit <u>hops</u> all around. He jumps high in the air.

9. I was <u>unhappy</u> when we lost the game. It made me feel sad.

10. Mike <u>enjoys</u> playing soccer. He likes to play all the time.

Grammar Minutes · Grade 1 © 2009 Creative Teaching Press

Minute 78

Name _____

For Numbers 1–5, read each pair of words. Write *Yes* if they are antonyms or *No* if they are not.

(**Hint**: Antonyms are words that mean the opposite.)

1. slow   fast   _____

2. happy   excited   _____

3. open   close   _____

4. in   inside   _____

5. start   stop   _____

For Numbers 6–10, read each set of words. Circle the two antonyms in each set.

6. young   old   child

7. push   tug   pull

8. hard   solid   soft

9. clean   dirty   fresh

10. right   up   left

Antonyms

Grammar Minutes · Grade 1 © 2009 Creative Teaching Press

Minute 79

Name _____

For Numbers 1–6, circle the correct antonym for the underlined word in each sentence.

1. Bobby is <u>on</u> the chair.   above   off

2. The <u>fat</u> cat belongs to Casey.   thin   big

3. The dog was <u>wet</u> after his bath.   clean   dry

4. Please <u>close</u> the door.   open   take

5. It was a bright and sunny <u>day</u>.   light   night

6. We <u>start</u> school early in the morning. end   begin

For Numbers 7–10, match each word on the left with its correct antonym on the right.

7. huge   **a.** new

8. fast   **b.** pretty

9. ugly   **c.** tiny

10. old   **d.** slow

Grammar Minutes • Grade 1 © 2009 Creative Teaching Press

Minute 80

Name _____

For Numbers 1–6, read each pair of words. Write *Yes* if they sound alike or *No* if they do not.
(**Hint**: Homophones are words that sound the same but are spelled differently and have different meanings.)

1. hi   high   _____

2. say   saw   _____

3. son   sun   _____

4. be   bee   _____

5. man   mean   _____

6. to   two   _____

For Numbers 7–10, match each word on the left with a word on the right that sounds like it.

7. by   **a.** blew

8. ate   **b.** see

9. blue   **c.** eight

10. sea   **d.** buy

Homophones

Minute 81

Name _____

For Numbers 1–5, read each pair of sentences. Circle the homophones in each pair.
(**Hint**: You must circle one word in each sentence.)

1. We wear blue pants to school. I don't know where we got them.

2. I know the answer to the question. The answer is "no."

3. My dad sent me to buy candy. I had one cent left.

4. I can't hear the baby. Bring him here to me.

5. The turtles swim in the sea. I see them every morning.

For Numbers 6–10, read each set of words. Circle the two words that sound alike in each set.

6. so   sew   saw

7. knew   knee   new

8. four   fire   for

9. dare   deer   dear

10. meet   might   meat

Grammar Minutes • Grade 1 © 2009 Creative Teaching Press

Minute 82

Name _____

For Numbers 1–5, circle the correct compound word for the two underlined words in each sentence.

1. A <u>fish</u> shaped like a <u>star</u>.   starfish   fishstar

2. A <u>room</u> with a <u>bed</u> in it.   roombed   bedroom

3. A <u>bell</u> for the <u>door</u>.   belldoor   doorbell

4. A <u>house</u> for a <u>bird</u>.   birdhouse   housebird

5. A <u>bird</u> that is <u>black</u>.   birdblack   blackbird

For Numbers 6–10, write a compound word with two words from each sentence.

6. The ball is made of snow.   _____

7. The boat has a sail.   _____

8. The shine comes from the sun.   _____

9. This lace is for my shoe.   _____

10. I have a box full of sand.   _____

Grammar Minutes · Grade 1 © 2009 Creative Teaching Press

Compound Words Review

Minute 83

Name _____

For Numbers 1–5, write the two words that make up each contraction.

1. she's _____ _____

2. we're _____ _____

3. shouldn't _____ _____

4. don't _____ _____

5. I'm _____ _____

For Numbers 6–10, write the contraction to best complete each sentence.

6. Mark said _____ not hungry.
   he's   she's

7. _____ eat candy before dinner.
   Shouldn't   Don't

8. My brother _____ read yet.
   can't   isn't

9. The movie _____ started.
   haven't   hasn't

10. The teacher told us _____ good students.
   we're   I'm

Grammar Minutes • Grade 1 © 2009 Creative Teaching Press

Minute 84

Name _____

Write _S_ if the pairs of words are synonyms or _A_ if they are antonyms.
(**Hint**: Remember that synonyms are words that mean the same thing, and antonyms are words that mean the opposite.)

1. on off _____

2. happy excited _____

3. early late _____

4. sad happy _____

5. nice sweet _____

6. buy sell _____

7. easy hard _____

8. mad angry _____

9. fast slow _____

10. tall high _____

Grammar Minutes · Grade 1 © 2009 Creative Teaching Press

Synonyms and Antonyms Review

Minute 85

Name _____

Write the correct word to complete each sentence.

1. The eagle _____ high in the sky.

flu   flew

2. I want you to _____ my family.

meat   meet

3. The _____ is full of beautiful fish.

see   sea

4. You have one _____ to finish your homework.

our   hour

5. I _____ first place in the contest.

one   won

6. The mouse ate the _____ piece of cheese.

whole   hole

7. Lana got dirt in her _____.

eye   I

8. His _____ is in the first grade.

son   sun

9. My dog chases his own _____.

tale   tail

10. _____ you like to come with us?

Would   Wood

Grammar Minutes • Grade 1 © 2009 Creative Teaching Press

Minute 86

Name _____

Circle the mistake in each sentence, and rewrite it correctly on the line.
(**Hint**: There is only one mistake in each sentence to correct.)

1. Ryan asked why we didn't invite he.   _____

2. The foxs were chasing the rabbit.   _____

3. The childs were excited about the fair.   _____

4. Marys sister was born in this hospital.   _____

5. Brittany love to climb trees.   _____

6. Mary seen her favorite movie last night.   _____

7. The five goose were swimming in the pond.   _____

8. Rebecca and i love ice cream.   _____

9. We picked the name kim for my hamster.   _____

10. My doctor's name is Dr. johnson.   _____

Grammar Minutes · Grade 1 © 2009 Creative Teaching Press

Apply Your Grammar Knowledge

Minute 87

Name _____

For Numbers 1–5, circle the proper name for a person in each sentence.
(**Hint**: There is one proper name, or noun, for a person in each sentence.)

1. Alana types fast on the computer.

2. Soccer is Martha's favorite sport.

3. Did you know that Justin is my cousin?

4. Tori washes her dog in the bathtub.

5. The librarian asked David to stop running.

For Numbers 6–10, circle the noun (naming word) and underline the verb (action word) in each sentence.

6. Dinosaurs lived very long ago.

7. Our kites flew higher than ever.

8. The kids yelled all of a sudden.

9. My cat doesn't eat a lot anymore.

10. Why won't the young boy talk?

Grammar Minutes · Grade 1 © 2009 Creative Teaching Press

Minute 88

Name _____

Circle the describing words in each sentence.
(**Hint**: Each sentence has two describing words to circle.)

1. He wore a blue tie with the black suit.

2. The red house on the corner is big.

3. There are seven apples in the white bowl.

4. I grow yellow corn in my huge garden.

5. The loud noise scared the little girl.

6. I like sour and sweet flavors.

7. Cool water feels fresh during the summer.

8. The slimy snail slid across the hard ground.

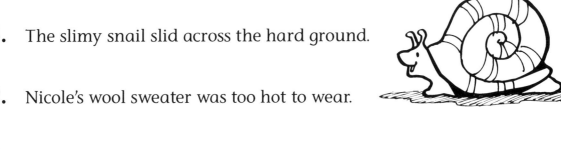

9. Nicole's wool sweater was too hot to wear.

10. The soft blanket was made of pink yarn.

Apply Your Grammar Knowledge

Minute 89

Name _____

For Numbers 1–6, circle the nouns in each sentence that should begin with capital letters.
(**Hint**: Each sentence has two words that should begin with capital letters.)

1. amy went to hannah's house for dinner.

2. kira lives in the state of nevada.

3. john works at grant Park on the weekends.

4. We will be on vacation in july and august.

5. i want to visit japan some day.

6. Next friday is the big halloween party.

For Numbers 7–10, rewrite each sentence correctly on the line.
(**Hint**: There are two mistakes in each sentence to correct.)

7. Mrs. kim comes on wednesdays.

_____

8. We went to hills museum yesterday.

_____

9. Our cats mars and duke are playful.

_____

10. mr. brady has six children.

_____

Grammar Minutes · Grade 1 © 2009 Creative Teaching Press

Minute 90

Name _____

Write the correct punctuation mark for the ending of each sentence.

1. My dad just won a brand-new car ____

2. Grace ate a hamburger for lunch ____

3. Do you want another glass of milk ____

4. I shopped for new shoes yesterday ____

5. What time is it ____

6. Don't you ever do that again ____

7. The cows are on the field ____

8. Amy is taking piano lessons ____

9. How are we going to get there ____

10. Heather is in bed reading a book ____

Apply Your Grammar Knowledge

Grammar Minutes · Grade 1 © 2009 Creative Teaching Press

Minute 91

Name _____

For **Numbers 1–5,** read each pair of sentences. Circle the correct sentence in each pair.

1. **a.** Her is trying to win a contest.
    b. She is trying to win a contest.

2. **a.** We cant start the show without them.
    b. We can't start the show without them.

3. **a.** We are waiting for you.
    b. Us are waiting for you.

4. **a.** Larry and Jake is not happy.
    b. Larry and Jake are not happy.

5. **a.** I had an egg and cheese sandwich.
    b. I had a egg and cheese sandwich.

For **Numbers 6–10,** circle the mistake in each sentence, and rewrite it correctly on the line.

6. Gary were late for school.   _____

7. The apple pie taste sweet.   _____

8. Ralph took John with he.   _____

9. Them are going to the dance.   _____

10. The clown has a read nose.   _____

Grammar Minutes · Grade 1 © 2009 Creative Teaching Press

Minute 92

Name _____

Read each group of words. Write *C* if each group of words is a complete sentence or *I* if it is incomplete.

1. Jack rescues the cat from the tree. _____

2. Myra cooks every night. _____

3. The elephants. _____

4. Kim spends all her money on pens. _____

5. Patsy puts grape jelly on her bread. _____

6. The hurt puppy. _____

7. Crawls on the floor. _____

8. Paula hopes it will not rain. _____

9. The balloons are too big. _____

10. The tiger in the tree. _____

Grammar Minutes · Grade 1 © 2009 Creative Teaching Press

Apply Your Grammar Knowledge

Minute 93

Name _____

For Numbers 1–5, circle whether each sentence is missing a *Noun* or a *Verb*.

1. The monkey _____ two bananas.   Noun   Verb

2. Larry's new _____ is lost.   Noun   Verb

3. Glenn _____ the guitar and drums.   Noun   Verb

4. Brad _____ three apples into the air.   Noun   Verb

5. Dorothy keeps her books on a _____.   Noun   Verb

For Numbers 6–10, use a word from the box to complete each sentence. Use each word only one time.

| Susan | marched | me | make | orange |

6. The _____ cat doesn't have a home.

7. Spiders _____ webs to catch food.

8. _____ waited for the school bus.

9. The band _____ across the football field.

10. Those gifts belong to my sister and _____.

Grammar Minutes · Grade 1 © 2009 Creative Teaching Press

Minute 94

Name _____

For Numbers 1–5, read each set of words. Circle the two homophones in each set.

(**Hint:** Remember that homophones are words that sound the same but are spelled differently and have different meanings.)

1. tail   tale   tall

2. raise   rose   rows

3. road   ride   rode

4. sale   safe   sail

5. pair   park   pear

For Numbers 6–10, read each pair of sentences. Circle the homophones in each pair.

(**Hint:** You must circle one word in each sentence.)

6. I am going to the market. I need two tomatoes.

7. Patty flew to Iowa. She got the flu there.

8. I will pick clothes to wear. Then I will close my closet.

9. He was sick all last week. He felt very weak and tired.

10. I would like to make a birdhouse. I need some wood.

Grammar Minutes · Grade 1 © 2009 Creative Teaching Press

Apply Your Grammar Knowledge

Minute 95

Name _____

Circle the mistake in each sentence, and rewrite it correctly on the line.
(**Hint**: There is only one mistake in each sentence to correct.)

1. I had a apple with my lunch.   _____

2. Him is sitting on the beach blanket.   _____

3. Mario and me are not going to the game.   _____

4. The cat chasing the mouse last night.   _____

5. Katie brush her teeth three times a day.   _____

6. Kela has a new pair of glass.   _____

7. Martin wear a sweater to school.   _____

8. Chloe are not in school today.   _____

9. Them are leaving the movies early.   _____

10. I is not ready for the test.   _____

Grammar Minutes • Grade 1 © 2009 Creative Teaching Press

Minute 96

Name _____

Write *Yes* if each sentence is correct or *No* if it is not.

1. I ate a hotdog, chips, and cake for lunch. _____

2. The jackson family is going to New Orleans. _____

3. jump high in the air Tommy can. _____

4. The fence needs to be painted. _____

5. The vase fell off the table. _____

6. The play was on January 15 2008. _____

7. The top of the hill was high. _____

8. Mary readed ten books in one weak. _____

9. We were glad when our noisy neighbors moved. _____

10. Kites are fun to flew. _____

Apply Your Grammar Knowledge

Minute 97

Name _____

For Numbers 1–5, write *Yes* if each set of words is in ABC order or *No* if it is **not**.

1. water, hair, ice _____

2. book, train, truck _____

3. pea, flea, tea _____

4. apple, banana, grapes _____

5. crayon, eraser, pencil _____

For Numbers 6–10, put each set of words in ABC order.

6. milk, pan, egg _____

7. snake, lion, pig _____

8. red, blue, pink _____

9. two, three, one _____

10. write, color, draw _____

Grammar Minutes · Grade 1 © 2009 Creative Teaching Press

Minute 98

Name _____

Circle the mistake in each sentence, and rewrite it correctly on the line.
(**Hint**: There is only one mistake in each sentence to correct.)

1. Us went to my grandmother's house. _____

2. There are ate children on the team. _____

3. Please wash the dishs. _____

4. My mother is a pretty women. _____

5. The five child are playing with the dog. _____

6. These three branch must come down. _____

7. I no where the party is going to be. _____

8. Samantha house is next door. _____

9. Why is you going there? _____

10. I can swam five laps in my pool. _____

Apply Your Grammar Knowledge

Minute 99

Name _____

Write the describing word that best completes each sentence.

1. An elephant is much _____ than a tiger.
      big   bigger   biggest

2. My dad's truck is the _____ one in the car show.
      nice   nicer   nicest

3. A bunny is _____ than a snake.
      soft   softer   softest

4. Our big dog barks much _____ than our small dog.
      loud   louder   loudest

5. That was the _____ movie I ever saw.
      scary   scarier   scariest

6. That pig is the _____ animal on the farm.
      fat   fatter   fattest

7. My hair is _____ than my sister's hair.
      dark   darker   darkest

8. He is the _____ kid I have ever met.
      mean   meaner   meanest

9. This sweater is _____ than that one.
      warm   warmer   warmest

10. The lemonade tastes _____ with sugar in it.
      sweet   sweeter   sweetest

Grammar Minutes • Grade 1 © 2009 Creative Teaching Press

Minute 100

Name _____

Write the correct present and past tense form in each sentence.

Present Tense	Past Tense

1. She _____ her bike
         rides   rode
 every day.
	2. She _____ her bike
	         rides rode
	 yesterday.

3. My dad _____ us
         makes   made
 dinner sometimes.
	4. My dad _____
	         makes made
	 dinner all last week.

5. We usually _____
         eat   ate
 dinner early.
	6. Last night we _____
	         eat ate
	 dinner late.

7. The singer _____
         writes   wrote
 her own songs.
	8. She even _____
	         writes wrote
	 a song for her mother.

9. Maria never _____
         loses   lost
 anything.
	10. Maria never _____
	         loses lost
	 anything before.

Apply Your Grammar Knowledge

Minute Answer Key

Minute 1
1. cap
2. gap
3. lap
4. map
5. nap
6. rap
7. sap
8. tap
9. yap
10. zap

Minute 2
1. gap
2. get
3. go
4. can
5. cop
6. cut
7. bat
8. bed
9. bit
10. bug

Minute 3
1. Yes
2. No
3. No
4. Yes
5. Yes
6. No
7. Yes
8. No
9. No
10. Yes

Minute 4
1. My
2. I
3. The
4. Susan
5. He
6. Birds
7. How
8. She
9. Candy
10. Danny

Minute 5
1. .
2. ?
3. .
4. !
5. ?
6. .
7. !
8. .
9. ?
10. ?

Minute 6
1. Complete
2. Not Complete
3. Complete
4. Not Complete
5. Complete
6. Complete
7. Not Complete
8. Complete
9. Complete
10. Not Complete

Minute 7
1. a
2. b
3. b
4. b
5. a
6. b
7. b
8. a
9. b
10. a

Minute 8
1. T
2. A
3. A
4. E
5. T
6. E
7. T
8. A
9. E
10. T

Minute 9
1. The circus
2. Tori and Cindy
3. My mother
4. John
5. The boy
6. Spiders
7. The clouds
8. Mackenzie and Kayln
9. I
10. The birds

Minute 10
1. works in the yard.
2. rakes the leaves.
3. watches us play.
4. jump into the leaves.
5. chases me.
6. picks up trash.
7. mows the grass.
8. makes lunch.
9. eat when we are done.
10. looks nice.

Minute 11
1. ant
2. bird
3. bug
4. cat
5. dog
6. duck
7. fish
8. fox
9. ox
10. pig

Minute 12
1. a
2. b
3. a
4. a
5. b
6. !
7. .
8. ?
9. .
10. ?

Minute 13
1. Not Complete
2. Complete
3. Complete
4. Not Complete
5. My kitten is white.
6. I like to read stories.
7. Our teacher is funny.
8. A
9. E
10. T

Minute 14
1. Chris
2. The candle
3. The bat
4. My parents
5. Mr. Paul
6. chases the cat.
7. hops away.
8. sits on the flower.
9. tells funny stories.
10. jumps up.

Minute 15
1. Nia
2. baby
3. teacher
4. Ryan
5. woman
6. mother
7. Sarah
8. mailman
9. zookeeper
10. Shawn

Minute 16
1. school
2. classroom
3. library
4. cafeteria
5. bathroom
6. outside
7. playground
8. office
9. yard
10. store

Minute 17
1. crayons
2. story
3. coat
4. milk
5. scissors
6. clock
7. homework
8. money
9. dress
10. paper

Minute 18
1. birds
2. cat
3. otter
4. dog
5. monkeys
6. cow
7. shark
8. lion
9. puppy
10. camel

Minute 19
1. Ms. Watson
2. Debra Hill
3. Dr. Young
4. Uncle Max
5. Principal Jones
6. Mike James
7. Coach Jenkins
8. Mrs. Patrick
9. Aunt Meg
10. Grandpa Joe

Minute 20
1. Stone Park
2. Douglas Street
3. Simmons School
4. Burger Hut
5. Candy Mall
6. Texas
7. New York
8. Martin Airport
9. Flower Trail
10. Disneyland

Minute Answer Key

Minute 21
1. Ming
2. Oscar
3. Roxy
4. Shimmer
5. Venom
6. Duke
7. Fluffy
8. Muffin
9. Simon
10. Nella

Minute 22
1. Saturday
2. June
3. Easter
4. July
5. September
6. Friday
7. Valentine's
8. October
9. Tuesday
10. April

Minute 23
1. May 28, 2006
2. February 12, 1996
3. April 16, 1980
4. November 1, 2008
5. June 15, 2009
6. No
7. Yes
8. No
9. Yes
10. Yes

Minute 24
1. Madison, Wisconsin
2. Columbus, Ohio
3. Selma, Alabama
4. Houston, Texas
5. San Francisco, California
6. Seattle, Washington
7. Atlanta, Georgia
8. Miami, Florida
9. San Diego, California
10. New York, New York

Minute 25
1. Apples, bananas
2. girl, sisters
3. students, playground
4. friend, bike
5. class, library
6. desks, chairs
7. cat, rug
8. flowers, garden
9. flashlight, room
10. food, party

Minute 26
1. Thing
2. Place
3. Person
4. Place
5. Animal
6. Person
7. Thing
8. Animal
9. Person
10. Animal

Minute 27
1. Virginia
2. John
3. February
4. Saturday
5. Halloween
6. Maria
7. Carter
8. Choco
9. Monday
10. Newport

Minute 28
1. April 2, 2009
2. March 15, 2008
3. June 1, 2010
4. December 20, 2006
5. September 30, 2009
6. Hollywood, California
7. Portland, Oregon
8. Tucson, Arizona
9. Denver, Colorado
10. Chicago, Illinois

Minute 29
1. sings
2. reads
3. play
4. say
5. grows
6. give
7. swim
8. rises
9. skips
10. picks

Minute 30
1. clap
2. love
3. fall
4. help
5. jumps
6. fly
7. eat
8. blows
9. make
10. run

Minute 31
1. pets
2. chops
3. bakes
4. paints
5. chases
6. plays
7. makes
8. runs
9. licks
10. barks

Minute 32
1. played
2. smelled
3. pulled
4. watched
5. jumped
6. cooked
7. asked
8. looked
9. named
10. painted

Minute 33
1. am
2. Are
3. is
4. are
5. are
6. am
7. is
8. are
9. are
10. is

Minute 34
1. was
2. were
3. was
4. was
5. were
6. was
7. were
8. was
9. were
10. was

Minute 35
1. No
2. Yes
3. Yes
4. Yes
5. No
6. No
7. No
8. Yes
9. Yes
10. Yes

Minute 36
1. cars
2. songs
3. beds
4. pets
5. planes
6. streets
7. bugs
8. books
9. games
10. trees

Minute 37
1. foxes
2. dishes
3. couches
4. bushes
5. glasses
6. buses
7. watches
8. boxes
9. beaches
10. classes

Minute 38
1. hills
2. peaches
3. circuses
4. spoons
5. wishes
6. hands
7. axes
8. coins
9. branches
10. birds

Minute 39
1. eat
2. pet
3. paints
4. ran
5. grew
6. went
7. melted
8. go
9. walked
10. takes

Minute 40
1. Past
2. Present
3. Present
4. Past
5. Present
6. Present
7. Past
8. Past
9. Present
10. Past

Minute Answer Key

Minute 41
1. had
2. were
3. is
4. am
5. are
6. is
7. had
8. have
9. was
10. has

Minute 42
1. cows
2. cups
3. witches
4. pails
5. foxes
6. hats
7. girls
8. dishes
9. stores
10. wishes

Minute 43
1. I
2. me
3. me
4. I
5. me
6. I
7. me
8. I
9. I
10. me

Minute 44
1. her
2. her
3. She
4. she
5. her
6. She
7. her
8. She
9. her
10. her

Minute 45
1. He
2. He
3. him
4. him
5. He
6. He
7. him
8. He
9. He
10. him

Minute 46
1. They
2. They
3. them
4. They
5. them
6. them
7. They
8. They
9. them
10. They

Minute 47
1. We
2. us
3. us
4. We
5. us
6. No
7. Yes
8. No
9. No
10. Yes

Minute 48
1. little
2. tall
3. big
4. long
5. small
6. round
7. square
8. flat
9. oval
10. skinny

Minute 49
1. pink
2. two
3. blue
4. four
5. three
6. red
7. black
8. yellow
9. five
10. three

Minute 50
1. sweet
2. sour
3. spicy
4. clean
5. minty
6. yummy
7. tasty
8. rotten
9. creamy
10. stinky

Minute 51
1. soft
2. loud
3. fuzzy
4. hard
5. squeaky
6. silky
7. squealing
8. chirping
9. rough
10. sharp

Minute 52
1. taller
2. easier
3. bigger
4. hotter
5. older
6. longer
7. colder
8. faster
9. nicer
10. higher

Minute 53
1. strongest
2. smallest
3. oldest
4. funniest
5. longest
6. No
7. Yes
8. No
9. Yes
10. Yes

Minute 54
1. No
2. Yes
3. No
4. Yes
5. No
6. Yes
7. No
8. Yes
9. No
10. No

Minute 55
1. She
2. them
3. him
4. us
5. her
6. He
7. They
8. me
9. him
10. her

Minute 56
1. tall, spicy
2. dark, big
3. red, white
4. sweet, tall
5. warm, furry
6. black, rotten
7. one, two
8. square, soft
9. dark, chocolate
10. loud, quiet

Minute 57
1. longer
2. tallest
3. later
4. cutest
5. cleanest
6. taller
7. smallest
8. sweeter
9. nicer
10. loudest

Minute 58
1. Sally's
2. plane's
3. cat's
4. Dean's
5. Maria's
6. tree's
7. park's
8. computer's
9. bunny's
10. Becky's

Minute 59
1. Yes
2. No
3. Yes
4. Yes
5. No
6. c
7. d
8. a
9. e
10. b

Minute 60
1. makes
2. sings
3. talks
4. wag
5. washes
6. fly
7. loses
8. rides
9. run
10. drives

Minute Answer Key

Minute 61
1. hug
2. runs
3. plays
4. buy
5. bake
6. throws
7. blows
8. skips
9. read
10. make

Minute 62
1. children
2. elves
3. mice
4. geese
5. teeth
6. women
7. men
8. feet
9. people
10. leaves

Minute 63
1. children
2. shelves
3. teeth
4. lives
5. feet
6. men
7. wolves
8. women
9. geese
10. mice

Minute 64
1. saw
2. left
3. fed
4. lost
5. drank
6. wrote
7. ate
8. fell
9. swam
10. drove

Minute 65
1. made
2. wrote
3. fell
4. broke
5. took
6. saw
7. ran
8. ate
9. came
10. said

Minute 66
1. an
2. a
3. a
4. an
5. an
6. a
7. a
8. an
9. an
10. a

Minute 67
1. The
2. An or The
3. an or the
4. A or The
5. A or The
6. the
7. a
8. an or the
9. an
10. The

Minute 68
1. Maggie's
2. Carrie's
3. girl's
4. Bob's
5. dog's
6. No
7. Yes
8. Yes
9. No
10. Yes

Minute 69
1. swims
2. watched
3. like
4. dive
5. raced
6. wins
7. takes
8. washed
9. rings
10. does

Minute 70
1. More than one
2. One
3. One
4. More than one
5. More than one
6. Present
7. Past
8. Past
9. Present
10. Past

Minute 71
1. No
2. Yes
3. Yes
4. Yes
5. Yes
6. No
7. Yes
8. No
9. Yes
10. Yes

Minute 72
1. bedroom
2. backyard
3. shoelaces
4. sunshine
5. jellyfish
6. homemade
7. homework
8. grandchildren
9. breakfast
10. sidewalk

Minute 73
1. Yes
2. No
3. No
4. Yes
5. Yes
6. No
7. Yes
8. Yes
9. No
10. Yes

Minute 74
1. isn't
2. hasn't
3. don't
4. can't
5. won't
6. haven't
7. don't
8. shouldn't
9. won't
10. isn't

Minute 75
1. d
2. e
3. a
4. f
5. b
6. c
7. we're
8. you're
9. she's
10. I'm

Minute 76
1. happy
2. large
3. pretty
4. quick
5. shout
6. c
7. e
8. d
9. b
10. a

Minute 77
1. hot, warm
2. see, look
3. fat, thick
4. sleep, nap
5. kind, nice
6. close, shut
7. big
8. jumps
9. sad
10. likes

Minute 78
1. Yes
2. No
3. Yes
4. No
5. Yes
6. young, old
7. push, pull
8. hard, soft
9. clean, dirty
10. right, left

Minute 79
1. off
2. thin
3. dry
4. open
5. night
6. end
7. c
8. d
9. b
10. a

Minute 80
1. Yes
2. No
3. Yes
4. Yes
5. No
6. Yes
7. d
8. c
9. a
10. b

Minute Answer Key

Minute 81
1. wear, where
2. know, no
3. sent, cent
4. hear, here
5. sea, see
6. so, sew
7. knew, new
8. four, for
9. deer, dear
10. meet, meat

Minute 82
1. starfish
2. bedroom
3. doorbell
4. birdhouse
5. blackbird
6. snowball
7. sailboat
8. sunshine
9. shoelace
10. sandbox

Minute 83
1. she is
2. we are
3. should not
4. do not
5. I am
6. he's
7. Don't
8. can't
9. hasn't
10. we're

Minute 84
1. A
2. S
3. A
4. A
5. S
6. A
7. A
8. S
9. A
10. S

Minute 85
1. flew
2. meet
3. sea
4. hour
5. won
6. whole
7. eye
8. son
9. tail
10. Would

Minute 86
1. him
2. foxes
3. children
4. Mary's
5. loves
6. saw
7. geese
8. I
9. Kim
10. Johnson

Minute 87
1. Alana
2. Martha's
3. Justin
4. Tori
5. David
6. noun: dinosaurs; verb: lived
7. noun: kites; verb: flew
8. noun: kids; verb: yelled
9. noun: cat; verb: eat
10. noun: boy; verb: talk

Minute 88
1. blue, black
2. red, big
3. seven, white
4. yellow, huge
5. loud, little
6. sour, sweet
7. cool, fresh
8. slimy, hard
9. wool, hot
10. soft, pink

Minute 89
1. amy, hannah's
2. kira, nevada
3. john, grant
4. july, august
5. i, japan
6. friday, halloween
7. Mrs. Kim comes on Wednesdays.
8. We went to Hills Museum yesterday.
9. Our cats Mars and Duke are playful.
10. Mr. Brady has six children.

Minute 90
1. !
2. .
3. ?
4. .
5. ?
6. !
7. .
8. .
9. ?
10. .

Minute 91
1. b
2. b
3. a
4. b
5. a
6. was
7. tasted or tastes
8. him
9. They
10. red

Minute 92
1. C
2. C
3. I
4. C
5. C
6. I
7. I
8. C
9. C
10. I

Minute 93
1. Verb
2. Noun
3. Verb
4. Verb
5. Noun
6. orange
7. make
8. Susan
9. marched
10. me

Minute 94
1. tail, tale
2. rose, rows
3. road, rode
4. sale, sail
5. pair, pear
6. to, two
7. flew, flu
8. clothes, close
9. week, weak
10. would, wood

Minute 95
1. an
2. He
3. I
4. chased
5. brushes
6. glasses
7. wears or wore
8. is
9. They
10. am

Minute 96
1. Yes
2. No
3. No
4. Yes
5. Yes
6. No
7. Yes
8. No
9. Yes
10. No

Minute 97
1. No
2. Yes
3. No
4. Yes
5. Yes
6. egg, milk, pan
7. lion, pig, snake
8. blue, pink, red
9. one, three, two
10. color, draw, write

Minute 98
1. We
2. eight
3. dishes
4. woman
5. children
6. branches
7. know
8. Samantha's
9. are
10. swim

Minute 99
1. bigger
2. nicest
3. softer
4. louder
5. scariest
6. fattest
7. darker
8. meanest
9. warmer
10. sweeter

Minute 100
1. rides
2. rode
3. makes
4. made
5. eat
6. ate
7. writes
8. wrote
9. loses
10. lost